PYRAMIDS

Created by Gallimard Jeunesse,
Claude Delafosse,
and Philippe Biard
Illustrated by Philippe Biard

A FIRST DISCOVERY BOOK

Cartwheel
·B·O·O·K·S· ®

SCHOLASTIC INC.
New York   Toronto   London   Auckland   Sydney

In ancient Egypt, the people thought their kings (or pharaohs) were gods who would live again after death.

When the pharaoh died, his body was sealed inside a stone monument called a pyramid. It was designed by the pharaoh's architect.

Royal priests and scholars studied
the stars to decide how to position the
base of the pyramid. Each corner of the
base was perfectly lined up with stars,
facing east, west, north, and south.

Many pyramids were built in the desert
near the Nile River.
Thousands of people worked on them.

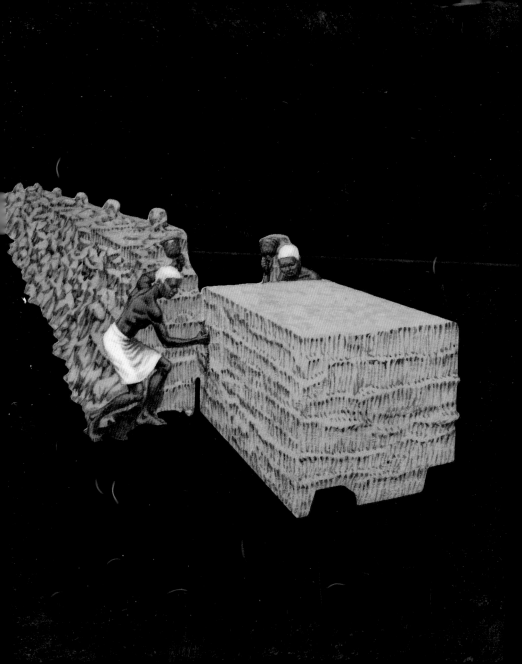

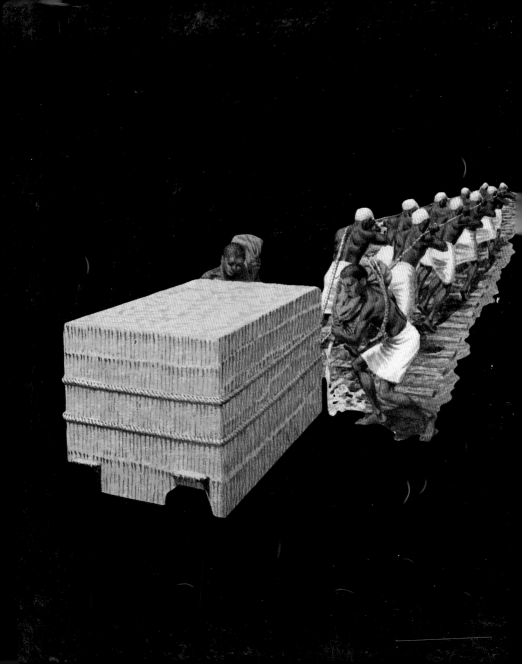

They cut huge stone
blocks in rock quarries.

The stone
blocks were
placed on
wooden
sledges and
pulled to
boats along a
watery track.

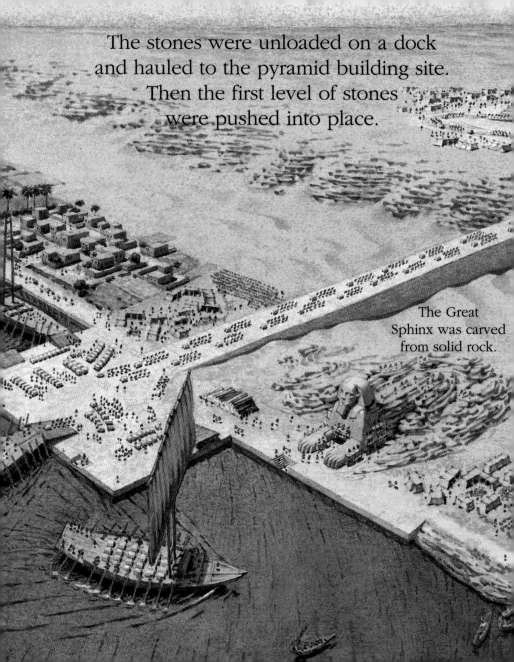

The stones were unloaded on a dock
and hauled to the pyramid building site.
Then the first level of stones
were pushed into place.

The Great
Sphinx was carved
from solid rock.

The stones that formed each new level of the
pyramid were pulled up along brick ramps,
built especially for this purpose.

Workers made bricks from mud and straw.

Later, when the pyramid was finished, all the brick ramps would be removed.

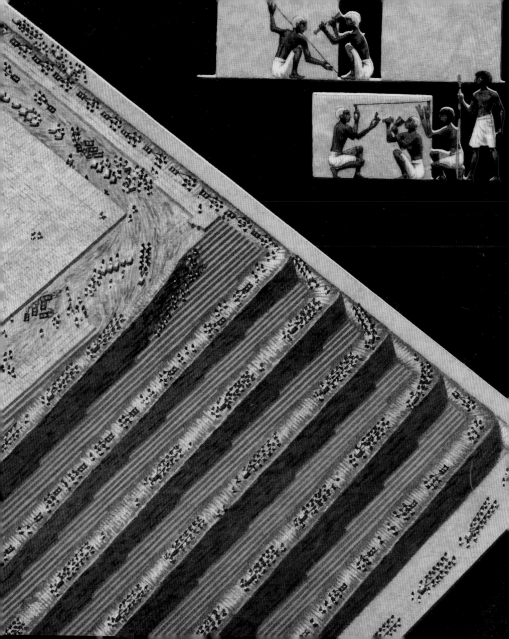

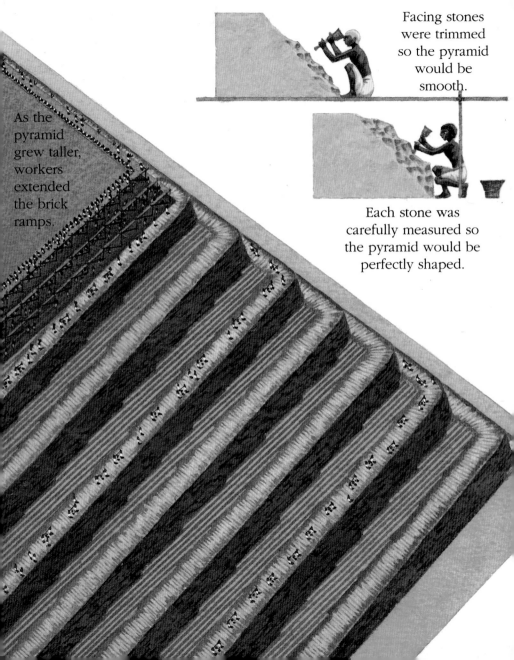

Facing stones were trimmed so the pyramid would be smooth.

As the pyramid grew taller, workers extended the brick ramps.

Each stone was carefully measured so the pyramid would be perfectly shaped.

The outer surface was covered
with polished limestone—
and finally, the pyramid
is finished.

Construction on
some pyramids,
such as the Great
Pyramid of King
Khufu, took more
than twenty years.
A hundred thousand
people worked on it!

More than two
million stone blocks
were used to build the
Great Pyramid. Some
weighed more than
two tons.

Inside, passageways were
built, leading to the tomb or
funeral chamber, where the
body of the pharaoh
would lie.

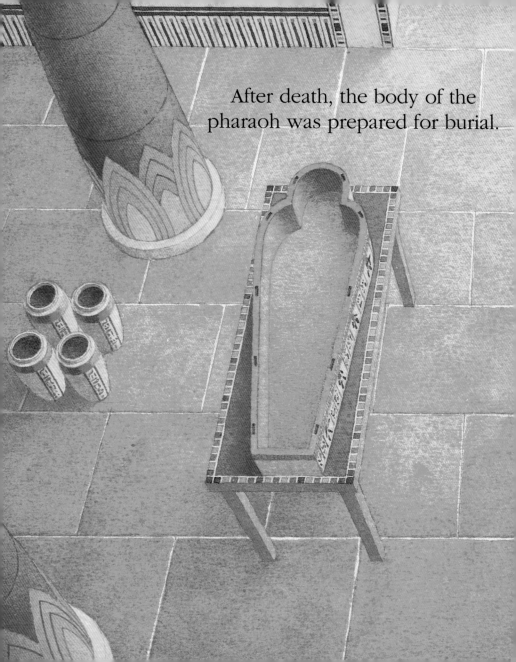

After death, the body of the pharaoh was prepared for burial.

The internal organs were removed
and placed in stone jars.
Then the body was cleaned, dried,
and wrapped in bandages.

The mummy was
placed inside a coffin
called a sarcophagus.

The
pharaoh's
family, priests,
and servants carried
the sarcophagus and the
king's treasures into the tomb.
Then the pyramid was sealed.

The Great Sphinx stands guard near the pyramid of King Khafre at Giza.

Originally, parts of the Sphinx were beautifully painted.

People believed the soul of the pharaoh flew up to rejoin the gods.

Today the Great Sphinx *still* stands, despite 4,000 years of damage from the harsh weather of the desert.

Over the ages, robbers broke into
the pyramids to steal the
valuable treasures.

To prevent such robberies, Egyptian pharaohs
began to choose burial in secret tombs
in a rocky area called the Valley of the Kings.
Even so, all but one of the royal tombs were robbed.

In 1922, a British archaeologist named
Howard Carter made a great discovery
in the Valley of the Kings.

He found the treasures of
King Tutankhamen hidden in a
tomb dug into a cliff.

And beyond the treasure chamber, Carter found
the mummy of King Tutankhamen himself!
Tutankhamen ruled Egypt from about 1361
until 1352 B.C. In over 3,000 years, his tomb
had never been robbed!

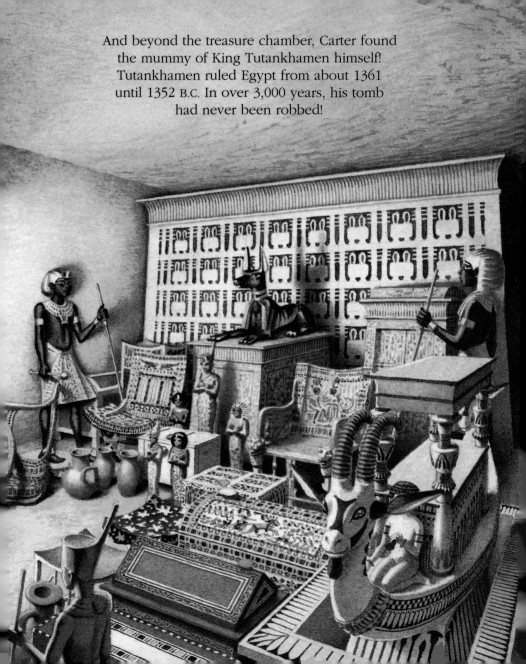

Ancient Pyramids of Egypt . . .

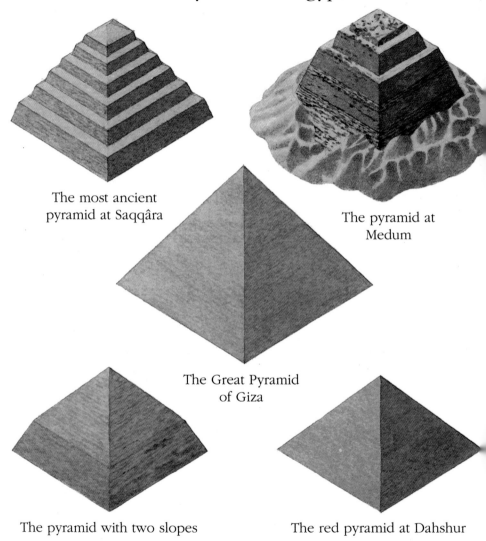

The most ancient
pyramid at Saqqâra

The pyramid at
Medum

The Great Pyramid
of Giza

The pyramid with two slopes

The red pyramid at Dahshur

Pyramids outside Egypt ...

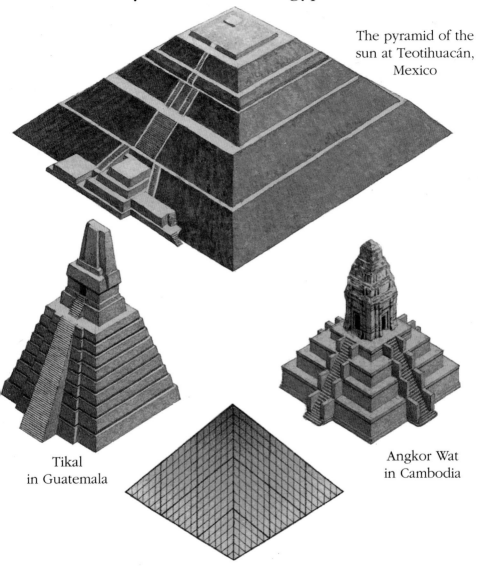

The pyramid of the sun at Teotihuacán, Mexico

Tikal
in Guatemala

Angkor Wat
in Cambodia

The glass pyramid at the Louvre Museum in Paris, France, was designed by architect I.M. Pei and completed in 1989.

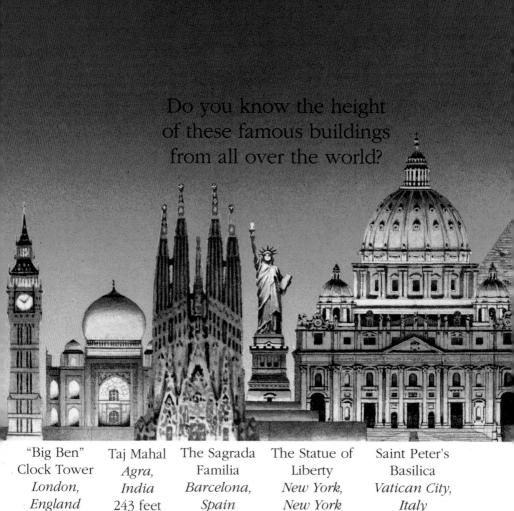

Do you know the height
of these famous buildings
from all over the world?

"Big Ben"
Clock Tower
London,
England
318 feet

Taj Mahal
Agra,
India
243 feet

The Sagrada
Familia
Barcelona,
Spain
361 feet

The Statue of
Liberty
New York,
New York
305 feet

Saint Peter's
Basilica
Vatican City,
Italy
433 feet

The Great
Sphinx
Giza, Egypt
66 feet

The Pyramid
of Khafre
Giza, Egypt
446 feet

The Ulm
Cathedral
Ulm, Germany
528 feet

The Eiffel
Tower
Paris, France
1046 feet

The Empire
State Building
*New York,
New York*
1469 feet

Here are the Seven Wonders of the Ancient World.

The Temple of Artemis at Ephesus (Turkey)

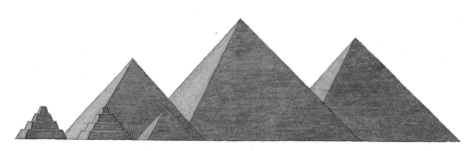

The pyramids at Giza (Egypt)

The Hanging Gardens of Babylon (Iraq)

The Mausoleum at
Halicarnassus (Turkey)

The Colossus of Rhodes
(Greece)

The statue of Zeus at
Olympia (Greece)

The Pharos (Lighthouse) at
Alexandria (Egypt)

Titles in the series of *First Discovery Books:*

**Airplanes
and Flying Machines**
All About Time
Bears
Birds
Winner, 1993
Parents Magazine
"Best Books" Award
Boats
Winner, 1993
Parents Magazine
"Best Books" Award
The Camera
Winner, 1993
Parents Magazine
"Best Books" Award
Castles
Winner, 1993
Parents Magazine
"Best Books" Award

Cats
Colors
Dinosaurs
The Earth and Sky
The Egg
Winner, 1992
Parenting Magazine
Reading Magic Award
Flowers   .
Fruit
**The Ladybug and
Other Insects**
Light
Musical Instruments
Pyramids
The Rain Forest
The River
Winner, 1993
Parents Magazine
"Best Books" Award

The Seashore
The Tree
Winner, 1992
Parenting Magazine
Reading Magic Award
Under the Ground
**Vegetables in the
Garden**
Weather
Winner, 1992
Oppenheim Toy Portfolio
Gold Seal Award
Whales
Winner, 1993
Parents Magazine
"Best Books" Award

Library of Congress Cataloging-in-Publication Data available.

Originally published in France under the title *La Pyramide* by Editions Gallimard.

ISBN 0-590-42786-5

12 11 10 9 8 7 6 5 4 3 2 1   5 6 7 8 9/9 0/0
Printed in Italy by Editoriale Libraria
First Scholastic printing, September 1995